Original title:
Chasing Life's Purpose (While Eating Cake)

Copyright © 2025 Creative Arts Management OÜ
All rights reserved.

Author: Elias Montgomery
ISBN HARDBACK: 978-1-80566-209-9
ISBN PAPERBACK: 978-1-80566-504-5

A Dash of Delight

In a world where frosting flows,
I ponder deep, as everyone knows.
With sprinkles bright and layers high,
I nibble thoughts, and here's my why.

While cake stands tall, I take a bite,
My worries fade, oh what a sight!
With every forkful, dreams arise,
A laugh erupts, beneath the skies.

Baking My Way Forward

I whisk my hopes with sugary cheer,
Each bite of cake, the path is clear.
Eggs and flour mix with fate,
I savor joys, it's never late.

With every bake, new plans emerge,
Butter and cream make visions surge.
As the oven hums a song so sweet,
I find my way, my heart's upbeat.

The Purposeful Plate

On this plate, ambitions sit,
Covered in icing, just a bit.
While others strive for goals so grand,
I take my spoon and make a stand.

With cake as fuel for dreams so bright,
I tackle tasks with pure delight.
Each slice I eat, a puzzle piece,
In this sweet game, I find my peace.

Dreams Baked in Time

In the kitchen, flour clouds the air,
I'm mixing hope with giggles to share.
Doughy dreams rise, soft and warm,
In this sweet space, I find my charm.

As time melts down with every bake,
I ponder joy, I laugh, I take.
With bites of life on sweetened lips,
My silly path is filled with quips.

Grease-Stained Journeys

With crumbs upon my shirt, I roam,
Pursuing pies in fields of foam.
Each bite brings me closer, I swear,
To wisdom baked with love and care.

Flour on my nose, I ponder deep,
While cupcakes tease me from their heap.
I laugh as frosting drips like rain,
In this sweet madness, I find my gain.

Flour Dust and Dreams

A whisk in hand, I set the pace,
For cake pursuits in this wild space.
Sprinkles fly like shooting stars,
Guiding me to my sweet memoirs.

Sifting doubts through a pan of cheer,
I mix my joys, then taste my fear.
With every slice, I find a way,
To savor life in my own sway.

Candied Hopes

I chase delight with icing gold,
Through sticky paths, both warm and bold.
Chocolate rivers, oh how they flow,
In candied hopes, I find my glow.

Each pastel dream a treat I seek,
Laughter bubbles, sweet and cheek.
With every bite, I feel alive,
In sugar's hug, I freely thrive.

The Confectionery Compass

A compass made of chewy sweets,
Directs my heart to tasty feats.
I navigate with frosting charts,
Exploring depths of doughy arts.

With every whisk and every fold,
New flavors blossom, tales unfold.
In the chaos of pies and laughs,
I find my way through dessert paths.

Whispers of Frosting and Dreams

A cupcake calls from far away,
Frosting swirls in bright array.
I ponder hard on why I stand,
With crumbs and sprinkles in my hand.

Each forkful bites of joys unknown,
A sugar high, my heart has grown.
I search for meaning in the glaze,
While icing drips in sweet malaise.

Slices of Intentions

A slice of laughter, a bite of fun,
Found in layers, I'm never done.
Each mouthful urges to explore,
As frosting whispers, 'There's so much more!'

Intentions bake beneath the heat,
While chocolate chips dance to the beat.
I ponder life with every crumb,
As cake calls out, 'Come on, let's hum!'

Crumbs of Clarity

In a tangle of frosting, I get lost,
What's the meaning? At what cost?
With every bite, I muse and sigh,
Where's the wisdom in frosting pie?

Crumbs of clarity fall in place,
Amidst the laughter, cake's embrace.
I giggle hard, not wanting to fret,
As dreams blend sweet on my palette yet.

The Sweet Pursuit

Oh, the quest for that perfect slice,
Each taste a sprinkle of paradise.
I chase the laughter, the sugary thrill,
With every mouthful, I feel the chill.

The sweet pursuit makes me quite bold,
With bites of wisdom barely told.
A cake-filled journey, oh what a ride,
Savoring life with frosting as my guide!

Sweet Moments of Discovery

In a bakery bright, with frosting in sight,
I ponder my fate, while munching with delight.
The cakes call to me, each flavor a clue,
To find what I seek, in chocolate and goo.

With a fork as my guide, I uncover the thrill,
Each slice brings me joy, can you feel the chill?
Banana or berry, what do I decide?
A sprinkle of wisdom, my cake, and my pride.

Icing on the Adventure

A cupcake parade, oh where do I start?
Each bite's a new quest, feeding my heart.
I travel the tiers, so fluffy and sweet,
With sprinkles of laughter, my journey's complete.

From lemon to coffee, with marshmallow dreams,
Life's a big party, or so it seems.
I dive into frosting, a whirl and a swirl,
Like a kid with a spoon, watch my joy unfurl.

The Recipe for Reflection

A whisk in my hand, I measure my fate,
With sugar and spice, I mix and create.
The oven's a portal, it beckons me near,
As vanilla fills the air, I grin ear to ear.

I ponder my choices, while flipping the cake,
What's on the menu? Oh, what will I bake?
Each layer a lesson, so rich and divine,
With cherries on top, everything's just fine.

A Dash of Purpose

In a world full of crumbs, I sift through the fun,
Life's recipe calls, mix in everyone.
A pinch of mischief, a dollop of cheer,
With cake as my compass, I'll conquer each year.

So let's eat our wishes, and bake with delight,
Whip dreams into batter, and take a big bite.
For every occasion, sprinkles galore,
In this tasty journey, who could ask for more?

Whisked Away in Wonder

In the kitchen, flour flies,
Mixing dreams with buttered sighs.
Recipes for laughter rise,
Life's a cake, a sweet disguise.

Batter spills, oh what a mess,
Stirring hopes, we must confess.
With every bite, we find success,
In sprinkles, joy, and no stress.

Slices of Serenity

A slice of peace, a bite of cheer,
Frosted moments we hold dear.
Sugar highs, wipe away the fear,
Each crumb whispers, 'Chill, my dear.'

Layers stacked with love and glee,
Flavors dance, just let it be.
Finding truth in calorie spree,
Cake's sweet wisdom sets us free.

Buttercream Reflections

In mirrors glazed with buttercream,
We ponder life with frosting dreams.
Life's a party, or so it seems,
With every slice, a new theme.

Whipped joy covers every doubt,
Sprinkled thoughts that twist about.
With cake in hand, we laugh and shout,
In sugary realms, we're never out.

The Quest for Joy Between Layers

Layers stacked with soft delight,
Searching for cheer, day and night.
In each nibble, a little fight,
Until it's gone, oh what a sight!

Craving crumbs of happiness,
Forks at the ready, no distress.
Every bite a close caress,
A sweet adventure we confess.

Cake and Clarity

In a world so wide and bright,
I seek a slice, just feels so right.
Frosting dreams and layers deep,
One more bite, just let me sleep.

Questions swirl like cream atop,
Whisking thoughts, I can't just stop.
Sprinkle wisdom with each taste,
Time's a layer, none to waste.

Indulgence in the Search

The quest for meaning, fun and sweet,
Sitting here with cake to eat.
Each forkful, a little clue,
Wrapped in chocolate, yum, oh goo!

With every crumb, I laugh and play,
Finding bliss in a creamy way.
Life's a party, bring the sweets,
Filling joy in fruity treats.

A Forkful of Intent

A fork in hand, I take my chance,
With buttercream, I start to dance.
Intentions mixed in batter rise,
Who knew that pie can also surprise?

Every bite a spark of fun,
Savoring life, I'm on the run.
With cake around, I find my path,
Laughing loud, it's all a laugh!

Sprinkling Hope on Every Bite

Hope's a sprinkle, sweet and bright,
Dust it on, all day, all night.
With every layer, dreams unfold,
In every slice, a tale retold.

Candied plans and creamy schemes,
Life's a layer cake of dreams.
So grab a slice and take a chance,
With laughter, we shall always dance!

An Oven of Opportunities

In the kitchen, dreams arise,
With flour flying through the skies.
A sprinkle here, a pinch of zest,
I bake my hopes, they bake the best.

Buttercream smiles and icing cheers,
Whisk away doubts, ignore the fears.
I bake my way through life's buffet,
One slice at a time, I'll find my way.

Layers of Longing

Each layer stacked, a wish concealed,
With chocolate dreams, my fate is sealed.
A cherry swirl on top of doubt,
I take a bite and scream out loud!

The world is just a giant slice,
I'll smudge my face with sugary vice.
The frosting sticks, but so does glee,
In every bite, there's part of me.

Forkfuls of Fate

With forks in hand, we improvise,
Savoring life, with sugary ties.
Each bite a choice, both bold and sweet,
A dessert dash, can't skip a treat!

Caramel drips, oh what a mess,
But sticky fingers mean good success.
Life's a buffet, I'll grab it all,
A giggle and crumb, let's have a ball!

Desserted Destinies

In whimsical kitchens, dreams collide,
With spatulas ready, there's no need to hide.
I swirl my fate with whipped cream flair,
Who knew life's lessons come in layers?

As cookies crumble, so do my plans,
But I'll sip my milk and lay my hands.
On frosted paths, I skip with glee,
Desserted destinies, just you and me!

Layered Aspirations

With forks in hand, we take a slice,
Each layer holds a sweet surprise.
We quest for dreams while crumbs fall free,
In laughter loud, we find our glee.

A sprinkle here, a frosting chase,
We wander through this sugary space.
Life's mixed up like batter in bowl,
But smiles arise, that's the goal.

So let us bake both joy and blunder,
As calories wash away our wonder.
In every flavor, a lesson learned,
For every burn, a dream returned.

And when the pie is all consumed,
We'll laugh about how we presumed.
With layers thick, we rise and swell,
Life's tastiest truths, we'll share and tell.

Cake and the Quest

On a journey paved with crumbs so sweet,
We wander far for the perfect treat.
With icing thick and layers high,
We leap for joy with every try.

The map is drawn in chocolate trails,
We sail through fudge and berry gales.
Each bite we take fuels our delight,
As frosting drips, we savor the bite.

A layer of dreams, a pinch of doubt,
We laugh our way, twirling about.
With each new slice, we chase the sun,
In frosting fights, we all have fun.

So gather round, let's share the cake,
While pondering what roads we'll take.
In this sweet quest, we'll find our way,
Through laughs and crumbs, we seize the day.

Frosted Pathways

On frosted paths, our feet will tread,
With sugary dreams that lie ahead.
We stumble, giggle, trip on cream,
In this sweet world, we form our team.

Each bite we take, a step to share,
Sprinkled hopes float in the air.
Chocolate rivers guide our way,
In laughter's echo, we joyfully play.

With jelly fills and caramel streams,
We dance along in icing dreams.
The road is sticky, but that's okay,
We'll rise with humor, come what may.

So let us bake our silly plight,
With every slice, we feel the light.
As calories blend with joyful cheer,
We find our path as we persevere.

A Recipe for Meaning

Combine a dash of whimsy bright,
With sprinkles of laughter, pure delight.
A cup of courage, mix it well,
In this sweet mix, we laugh and dwell.

Add dreams like eggs, and stir with care,
Fold in the moments, sweet and rare.
With frosting thick, we'll pile it high,
As flavors meld, our spirits fly.

The oven hums a cheerful tune,
As batter rises, we swoon and boon.
In this delight, we find our way,
Through sugar highs, we seize the day.

So bake with joy, and share the woes,
With every piece, a new path flows.
In every bite, we find our fate,
Life's recipe sweetens as we create.

Culinary Contemplations

With frosting on my face so grand,
I ponder dreams and what they mean.
A cupcake whispers, 'Take my hand,'
   As I debate my life on cream.

Each sprinkles' color tells a tale,
Of hopes and wishes, sweet and bright.
I wander through this sugary veil,
   Embracing joy with every bite.

The pie sits there, so round and warm,
Tempting thoughts of fate and fun.
In every slice, I find a charm,
   Perhaps my purpose weighs a ton?

One layer deeper, I must dive,
To discover what lies beneath.
A scone reminds me, just survive,
With tea to share, explore, and breathe.

Happiness in Every Bite

In a bakery with glee I stroll,
With every pastry, laughs arise.
Éclairs and tarts enhance my soul,
While pondering my funny ties.

Chocolate frosting, smooth and wide,
Says, "Life's short, so take a chance!"
I take a fork and dare to ride,
These layers bring a comical dance.

A donut's hole reflects my quest,
For meaning in this tasty trance.
Each bite feels like a joyous jest,
Inviting me to take a glance.

So here I stand, with cake in hand,
Unraveling life's sweet little tricks.
A sprinkle here, a giggle planned,
While savoring these fluffy kicks.

A Slice of Serenity

In quiet moments, cake's my muse,
Its layers whisper soft, profound.
I slice through doubts, I chuckle, snooze,
In buttery bliss, life's joys abound.

Cheesecake dreams with crusty bases,
Encourage thoughts of grace and cheer.
Its velvety tale runs through my aces,
As I attempt to face my fears.

A fork in hand, a laugh at fate,
Each morsel brings a brighter thought.
In every crumb, I celebrate,
The silly lessons life has taught.

So let me feast on whimsy's art,
As layers lift my spirit high.
With every nibble, Truth will start,
Beneath the sugar-coated sky.

Decadent Doctrines

In chocolate pools of thought, I float,
A fruit tart guides me with a wink.
I ponder life while smooth cream coats,
Each bite inviting me to think.

A gooey brownie speaks of fate,
With nuts that crunch like wisdom's voice.
As I devour, laugh, and sate,
I find my path, I have a choice.

Between the layers lies the fun,
As cupcakes giggle at my plight.
In frosting fights, I've just begun,
To mix my dreams, sweet and light.

So bring me sweets and silly quotes,
With each dessert, I'll twirl and glide.
In pastry wisdom, joy promotes,
As life unfolds, with cake beside.

The Flavor of Fulfillment

I forked my dreams with sweet delight,
Each bite a joy, a little light.
Sprinkles of hope on top I lay,
With every slice, I laugh and sway.

Mixing flour with plans unknown,
I bake my wishes, let them be grown.
A dash of sugar, a pinch of zest,
My quest for bliss is quite the fest.

Layers of Ambition

I stack my goals like a tower tall,
With icing swirls that never fall.
Each layer holds a dream, a laugh,
A recipe for joy, my autograph.

Whisking wishes in a bowl so wide,
Baking laughter, I take in stride.
With every slice, I piece together,
A cake of dreams to last forever.

Craving Connection and Cream

Frosting smiles as I share my bite,
To friends nearby, it feels so right.
Whipping up stories, sweet and fun,
With laughter echoing, hearts weigh a ton.

Creamy layers, friendships blend,
In this dessert, we find our mend.
A sprinkle here, a dollop there,
Together we savor, without a care.

Beyond the Oven: A Journey

From mixing bowls to golden crust,
In each adventure, we place our trust.
Hot from the oven, dreams take flight,
With every nibble, we feel just right.

Butter and sugar, united so bold,
A journey of flavors, new stories told.
With laughter rising like a cake so grand,
In this sweet life, we take a stand.

The Slice of Satisfaction

In a bakery bright, I seek my fate,
Countless confections on a silver plate.
With each sweet bite, I ponder the quest,
Life and dessert, I feel truly blessed.

Fork in hand, I dive right in,
Chocolate rivers, let the fun begin.
Layers of cream stacked high like dreams,
With each slice served, a giggle that beams.

What is my path? Is it vanilla or pie?
I ponder while munching, oh me, oh my!
Every crumb tells a story, delicious and true,
I laugh as I nibble, what else can I do?

So come join me here, let's frolic and feast,
In the land of the sweet, where worries decrease.
With frosting and laughs, we'll savor the play,
Life's sweet surprises lead us astray.

Savoring Our Stories

With each little bite, a tale unfolds,
Whisked dreams of sugar, the joy they hold.
Glimpses of laughter in frosting so bright,
Unexpected flavors, pure delight!

I scoop up the stories, each layer a laugh,
Mixing fond memories with a bubbly gaff.
Cheesecake giggles, pie crust scheming,
Life's complexities wrapped in sweet dreaming.

A canvas of cookies, glazed with hue,
What color defines the adventures I brew?
In frosting confessions, we find our way,
Savoring secrets, icing our play.

So gather around, let's dig in with glee,
A banquet of joy, just you and me.
With bites full of laughter, we'll sit and relate,
As sugar-coated stories are served on each plate.

Frosting in the Details

Life in between bites, oh what a ride,
Cakery dreams where we all confide.
Frosting so thick, it hides all the strife,
Within each layer, we discover our life.

Sprinkles of chaos dance on our tongue,
While eggs crack open, our adventure's begun.
Rising like dough, with hopes tucked inside,
We savor the sweetness in these tasty slides.

Whipped cream whispers of secrets to share,
In a slice of mischief, we find that we care.
With every bite softened by laughter and cheer,
Life's little treasures are so very near.

So grab a slice quick and let's set the stage,
Baking our memories, they're never too vague.
You'll find frosting wonders in details we trace,
In laughter we flourish, in sweetness, our grace.

Poetic Pastry Pursuits

With forks in our hands, we embark on a spree,
Pastries aplenty, just you wait and see!
The buttercream mountains are calling my name,
Each bite is a journey, an exquisite game.

I wrestle with cookies, they smirk and they cheer,
As I navigate dreams, one crumb at a cheer!
Tarts full of fruit parade on my plate,
Trying to catch joy before it's too late.

Life's a grand buffet, with ups and downs,
Yet in sugary moments, we wear joyful crowns.
Cake for breakfast? Why not, I say!
Let's dance through our choices in a sweet ballet.

Each pastry has stories, let's giggle and munch,
As icing cascades, let's savor our lunch.
What flavors unite us, what tales will ignite,
In poetic pursuits, let's dive in tonight.

Whipped Wishes

A slice of joy upon my plate,
I dream of dreams I'd love to sate.
With frosting thick, my goals do dance,
I munch away, not in a trance.

Sprinkles of hope on top do gleam,
I ponder life; what does it mean?
With every bite, I gain some cheer,
And more dessert, my path is clear!

I twirl my fork, a whisking fate,
Is fortune just a piece of cake?
I laugh out loud at all my schemes,
As icing drips, I chase my dreams.

Tiers of Existence

A cake stacked high, my dreams unfurl,
With layers rich, they spin and swirl.
The topmost tier, insight so sweet,
I pile on hopes, with frosting meet.

Each forkful sparks a quirky thought,
What lessons here are life forgot?
As crumbs cascade, I make a mess,
With every slice, I'm blessed, I guess!

In life's sweet oven, I do bake,
With giggles round each charming flake.
While munching still on fears I face,
I find my joy in frosting's grace.

Life Served on a Platter

A platter full of options bright,
I scoop up bliss, it feels so right.
With every nibble, dreams take flight,
I savor every single bite.

With cake so rich, I ponder true,
What really matters, me or you?
I lick the plate, with glee I shout,
Life's sweetest lessons never pout!

In tasty trials, I take the lead,
With frosted joy, I plant the seed.
Each forkful leads to silly fun,
In cake's embrace, I've really won!

Sugar-Coated Discoveries

With sugar dreams, the world does gleam,
In every slice, I find my theme.
A dash of giggles, a dash of truth,
In frosting's swirl, I find my youth.

Each cupcake holds a tale untold,
In chocolate rivers, I feel bold.
I dive on in, no fear in sight,
As frosting clouds ignite delight.

In every bite, a laugh I find,
With sugar rush, I clear my mind.
So here's a toast with cake ablaze,
To joyful paths in sweet arrays!

Morsels of Meaning

A slice of joy, a bite of bliss,
In frosting lands, I chase my wish.
With every chew, a dream takes flight,
Cake crumbs scatter, a spark of light.

Sprinkles dance like thoughts in air,
I map my path—I'm almost there!
But what's this taste? It's lemon zest,
A zany twist on my life's quest!

A fork in hand, I ask for more,
What lies ahead? A candy store!
Choco rivers call my name,
In cake quests, I seek my fame.

Each mouthful brims with laughter's sound,
And in each bite, new truths are found.
With pie and tart, I greet the day,
Through sugar highs, I find my way.

Sweet Pursuits of the Heart

With frosting thick, I set my sights,
On sugary dreams and tasty bites.
A cherry on top, a wink of fate,
I sprint toward sweets before it's late.

Who knew delight could spark such glee?
In every crumb, a mystery.
I ponder life with each new slice,
Is this the cake of sacrifice?

A cupcake's tale, a cookie's lore,
Each morsel whispers, 'There's so much more!'
In layers stacked, my fortune grows,
Not just in cake, but in what it shows.

With every bite, a laugh ensues,
Life's grand design in sprinkles and hues.
I dive into dessert, heart set to roam,
Finding purpose in the sweetest home.

Frosted Dreams and Meaning

A slice of pasta? Oh no, wait!
That's just my cake—I'm feeling great.
Each layer hides a lesson true,
In frosting dreams, what shall I do?

Perhaps a cupcake could reveal,
The secrets of my heart's appeal.
With every bite, I chew on fate,
And watch my worries dissipate.

In chocolate rivers, dip my spoon,
Creating joy beneath the moon.
Sprinkle wisdom on top, they say,
As I munch my doubts all away.

So let the laughter fill the air,
As I devour without care.
In every crumb, I take a dive,
Here's to the cake—my will to thrive!

The Crumbs of Destiny

In teacakes' dance, I find my way,
Through frosting fields I laugh and play.
A nibble here, a muffin there,
My mission sweet—who needs a prayer?

With every tart, new paths unfold,
A biscuit's tale, worth more than gold.
Around each fork, stories spin,
In dessert world's wild chagrin.

Crumb by crumb, I weave my dream,
With jolly giggles, laughter streams.
What's life's purpose? It's in my plate,
As I dig into delicious fate.

So here's to cake, the secret key,
Unlocking truth—or positive glee.
A spoonful joyous, a cupcake bright,
In baked delights, I see the light.

The Essence of Elegance

A slice of cake and dreams collide,
In layers sweet, we take a ride.
I ponder goals while eating crumbs,
As frosting glistens, here it comes.

With every bite, my thoughts expand,
A plan of sorts, I must withstand.
Cake in hand, I laugh and scheme,
Life's grand purpose, all a dream.

The candles flicker, light our way,
Forty wishes for this day.
But with each savor, I forget
What I was aiming for, you bet.

So here we stand, with crumbs galore,
A joyful heart, that's what it's for.
I swore I'd change the world today,
Yet here I am — just pass the tray!

Pastry and Purpose

In the kitchen, flour flies high,
With every mix, my spirits sigh.
What's my goal? Who even knows?
Oh look! A pastry! There it goes.

I roll the dough with glee and laugh,
Seeking answers in my craft.
While sugar dances in the bowl,
I find a purpose, in a roll.

My plans may crumble like the crust,
But icing makes it all a must.
For every slice that satisfies,
I find my truth, through sweetened highs.

So bring the forks, let's share a slice,
With zest for life, I'm feeling nice.
No need for maps, we've found our way,
In pastries rich, we'll seize the day!

The Sugar Rush of Life

A cupcake tower, tall and bright,
With sprinkles dancing in the light.
I ask, what's next? A joyful quest,
To munch and crunch — it feels the best.

As frosting swirls, my mind spins round,
With every bite, new truths are found.
A giggle here, a laugh, a cheer,
I find my purpose, oh so near.

The clock ticks on, but who's to care?
When chocolate calls, we're light as air.
Oh, life's a game, let's play it sweet,
With every taste, I find my beat.

So snack with glee, enjoy the ride,
In every nibble, we confide.
As crumbs fall softly on the floor,
We savor life, and then some more!

Bites of Benevolence

A pie of kindness, served with grace,
In every slice, a warm embrace.
I ponder life while passing treats,
With laughter, joy, and sugar beats.

I meet my friends, we slice and share,
With whipped cream piled high, we care.
Each mouthful rich, a moment stored,
In every crumb, our hearts adored.

What is this thing we seek to find?
A cake of joy to soothe the mind.
With every chuckle, every cheer,
We slice through doubts, let go of fear.

So gather 'round, let's feast tonight,
With pastry dreams, we take flight.
In bites of love, we stake our claim,
Together, we will share this game!

A Palate of Purpose

In search of meaning, I delight,
With frosting on my fork, I take a bite.
Each flavor whispers secrets, it's true,
Chocolate dreams, where to pursue?

A slice of lemon, tart and bright,
A hint of joy in sugary light.
With every nibble, I plot my quest,
Who knew that cake could be the best?

A cherry on top, my thoughts collide,
Between a crumb and a moment's pride.
A layer of laughter, stacked so high,
As crumbs of wisdom flutter by.

With icing smudged upon my face,
I savor both the cake and grace.
Through bites of bliss, I find my way,
Life's sweetest purpose, come what may.

Icing on the Horizon

A sprinkle here, a drizzle there,
Searching for dreams in the kitchen air.
With every slice, my spirit sings,
I wonder just what the next cake brings.

The buttercream clouds float in my mind,
A frosted fortune I hope to find.
With red velvet thoughts, so bold and bright,
I dance through flour, a silly sight.

Gazing at layers, tall as a tree,
What's the secret? Will it come to me?
A cup of laughter mixed with cheer,
As sprinkles of joy draw ever near.

Sifting through choices, I take a stand,
With cake in hand, I'm in command.
The horizon glimmers, sugar-coated dreams,
I find my purpose in buttery beams.

Sweet Endeavors

Flour clouds gather, oh what a mess,
The quest for purpose, a delightful stress.
With sugar comets flying about,
I giggle and scheme, without a doubt.

Each cupcake cheers as I make my way,
Finding life's meaning in every tray.
A frosted fate, I can't resist,
In sweet endeavors, I find my bliss.

Sprinkling smiles on my path ahead,
With every frosting swirl, I'm gently led.
Decisions like cookies, baked crisp and warm,
In this sweet life, I weather the storm.

So here's a wish on a cake platter,
That all my questions start to scatter.
In each tender bite, I'll raise a toast,
To sweet endeavors and what I love most.

Cakewalks through Existence

In a world of cake, I take a stroll,
With cookie crumbs that feed my soul.
Each flavor takes me, spinning round,
While icing puddles gather on the ground.

Wandering through layers, light as air,
I dance with cupcakes, merrily unaware.
With every giggle, I twirl and glide,
Through pastry-filled dreams, I take a ride.

Life's a cakewalk, sweet and absurd,
Where frosting's the anthem, constantly heard.
With each sweet step, I claim my delight,
Finding purpose in laughter, oh, what a sight!

So let us eat cake, sing and play,
In this whimsical search, come what may.
A sugar rush teaches me each day,
That joy is the frosting on life's display.

The Icing on the Path

I wander through the frosting haze,
With sprinkles bright and playful ways.
The quest for joy and sugary bliss,
A slice of life I surely miss.

With every crumb that falls apart,
I find a giggle, in my heart.
The road is paved with chocolate dreams,
Laughter bubbles, or so it seems.

I juggle forks and baking pan,
Balancing hopes with a cupcake plan.
Each step a bite, a daring leap,
In sugar-coated smiles, I creep.

So here I skip, with cake and cheer,
Life's sweet delight is always near.
With frosting dreams on every side,
I run, I laugh, and full I ride.

Bites of Bravery

In the kitchen of my wildest dreams,
I bake up courage with sweet whipped creams.
A layer of fear, I slice away,
With marshmallow fluff, I seize the day.

Each forkful taken is bold and brave,
I conquer each crumb, my spirit I save.
Sprinkling joy, I dash with zest,
In this cake-filled quest, I'm truly blessed.

Frosted wishes on every bite,
Life's messy, but it feels so right.
I'll savor sweetness, laugh in style,
And dance through frosting, mile by mile.

Through buttercream clouds, I will glide,
With giggles echoing, I take pride.
For every cake I make or taste,
I find my heart in layers laced.

Cake and Contentment

A plate of joy, so rich and round,
In every slice, happiness is found.
I nibble away at worries cake,
Finding peace in every bake.

Chocolate whispers call my name,
In vanilla sky, I stake my claim.
With each bite taken, I let out a cheer,
Life feels lighter with frosting near.

I twirl and spin, with crumbs in hand,
Living large in this pastry land.
With giggles spreading like icing thick,
I savor each moment, layer and lick.

In laughter's glow, I find my way,
With cake and smiles, I choose to stay.
So raise a slice, shout out loud,
In this frosted world, I feel so proud.

The Journey of Layers

Life's a cake, with layers deep,
In every slice, there's joy to keep.
I gather friends like fondant sweet,
Together we're strong, with laughter's beat.

I laugh at crumbs that scatter wide,
As frosting drips, I take it in stride.
In mixing bowls of brilliant dreams,
I bake my hopes, or so it seems.

With forks held high, we share our fate,
In each bite, there's never too late.
From rich to light, flavors entwine,
In this banquet of laughter, I dine.

So let's raise a glass, or maybe a plate,
For moments sweet that feel like fate.
In layers of cake, I find my truth,
With every laugh, I reclaim my youth.

Savoring the Sweet and Sour

In a kitchen where hopes swiftly rise,
Mixing flour with dreams and some sighs.
A dash of sugar, a sprinkle of glee,
Life's recipe calls, come bake it with me.

With butter that melts like our worries away,
We flip pancakes of doubt, come join in the play.
A frosting of laughter, let's coat it just right,
Savoring moments, oh what a delight!

Life's pie has its slices, sweet, sour, and weird,
Like grandmas who baked just to see us all cheered.
So let's take a bite, and we'll giggle and chime,
At how every flavor is seasoned with time.

A Slice of Tomorrow's Dreams

With forks made of whimsy, we tackle the cake,
Each bite a new dream, accompanied by ache.
Layers of laughter, whipped cream on the side,
Tomorrow's pie waiting, let's take it in stride.

There's frosting of wishes, a crumble of fears,
We sprinkle on giggles, like confetti in tears.
Every nibble reveals a sweet, silly thing,
Like finding true joy that the frosting can bring.

The cupcakes of chaos all dance on the plates,
While frosting debates if it's sugar or fates.
So slice out the weekend, we've nothing to lose,
Just savor the moment, while we take a snooze.

Mixed Ingredients of Existence

In a bowl of existence, mix laughter and fun,
Add a sprinkle of chaos, and we're never done.
A whip of imagination, some batter of doubts,
We bake up our joy, amidst giggles and shouts.

Quite the recipe, we measure with quirks,
Butter and sugar blend well with the smirks.
Let's frost our ambitions with colors so bright,
And munch through the madness, what a tasty bite!

The oven of chance preheats with delight,
Where cookies of courage pop up in the night.
We serve up our dreams on plates made of bliss,
And laugh at the moments we surely won't miss.

The Pan of Possibilities

In the pan of our dreams, we flip hopes with flair,
A splash of ambition, a sprinkle of care.
Baking the future with kindness and speed,
Each slice we consume plants a flavorful seed.

The batter is swirling with whims and some cheer,
A dash of resilience, it's safe to draw near.
Toppings of wisdom, icing of play,
Let's feast on the challenges that come our way.

So let's stir our ambitions, a delightful new batch,
With every bite taken, we find a new catch.
The pan of potential never runs dry,
As we nibble through life, we reach for the sky.

Whisking Wishes

In a kitchen bright with dreams,
I whisk my hopes like batter,
Flour flies in every beam,
As laughter is what truly matters.

Sprinkles on my thoughts galore,
Frosting on a mission high,
Each bite opens a new door,
Taste buds twinkling, oh my, oh my!

Blooming Buttercream

Buttercream blooms like spring,
While I ponder life's true zest,
Is it joy or just a fling?
My cake slice is my very best!

Petals of taste swirl in the air,
As visions of bliss unfold,
With every fork, I show I care,
In moments sweet, I feel bold.

Confections and Contemplation

Cupcakes lined in tasty rows,
Each a tiny life to lead,
Filling my heart while my mind flows,
On crumbs of thought, I do succeed.

Polka-dots of icing bright,
Amidst my musings, they're right there,
With every nibble, I take flight,
And find delight in buttery care.

Sweetness Found in the Struggle

Life's an oven, hot and wild,
With layers mixed in every fight,
I bake my dreams, like a child,
And savor moments filled with light.

When life gives lemons, add cake,
Let bittersweetness have its say,
With frosting on the path I make,
I giggle as I find my way!

Frosting on the Path

I set my sights on dreams galore,
A sprinkle here, a crumb to score.
With cake so sweet, it's hard to wait,
But first, let's frolic—hold that plate!

I tripped on fondant, had a laugh,
Mixing giggles with a splash of half.
Between the layers, life unfolds,
With every slice, new tales retold.

The candles flicker, joy ignites,
In frosting hues, I find my heights.
Each mouthful shared, a quest begun,
To find the fun before it's done.

So here I stand, a pie in hand,
With every bite, I make my stand.
Through frosting dreams, my spirit grows,
Life's purpose swirls in butter flows.

The Taste of Transformation

From batter thick, I rise and bake,
A pinch of hope, a generous cake.
I mix the flavors, stir my soul,
With every taste, I feel more whole.

Whisking doubts with sugar bright,
Giggles echo in the fading light.
Layers of laughter, a savory spree,
This frosted journey is just for me.

When life gets tough and forks are near,
I serve up joy, I persevere.
In every bite, a lesson learned,
Through all the laughs, my fire burned.

I savor each crumb, embrace the mess,
In sweet disarray, I find my zest.
So here I stand, a slice to share,
Transforming life with cake and care.

Baking the Unseen

In the oven's warmth, dreams start to rise,
With flour clouds and hopeful sighs.
I toss in smiles, a dash of cheer,
For every moment, I hold dear.

Baking secrets just out of sight,
Like little treasures in twilight.
Each epic fail, a doughy mess,
Taught me that fun is a grand success.

I roll with laughter, I knead with flair,
In this odd kitchen, I find my air.
Through buttered whispers and chocolate streams,
I mix my purpose with tasty dreams.

So grab the spatula, join the dance,
With every layer, I take my chance.
Life's recipes may go awry,
But sweetened chaos makes me fly!

Savory Steps toward Significance

With forks in hand, we take a bite,
Life's recipe is pure delight.
In every nibble, wisdom grows,
Through tasty treats, a spirit glows.

We measure moments, mix and pour,
Laughter spilling onto the floor.
With sprinkles scattered, we make our way,
Through layers of life, we laugh and play.

In this sweet journey, we dance and spin,
With crumbs of joy as we begin.
We gather round, a cake parade,
Finding meaning in every trade.

So let's embrace this scrumptious quest,
With frosted dreams, we'll be our best.
Among the layers, we learn and share,
In savory steps, we claim our flair.

Journey of a Thousand Crumbs

With frosting on my nose, I roam,
In search of dreams, my sugary home.
The cake may wobble, but so do I,
Two bites in, and I'm ready to fly.

A layer of laughter, sweetened delight,
Each slice a step, though the path's not quite right.
I stumble on sprinkles, my heart's full of cheer,
This frosting adventure makes everything clear.

Rolling like dough, through layers I sift,
Onward I march, an adventurer's gift.
With crumbs in my pockets and glee on my face,
I'll conquer all doubts, one forkful, one chase.

So here's to the journeys that lead to the bite,
With each spin of the whisk, my spirit takes flight.
Though paths may be messy, there's joy in the cake,
Each crumb tells a story—make no mistake!

Taste Buds and Truths

In the land of sprinkles, I seek out the best,
With each taste I find, my soul gets a quest.
A chocolate eruption, a caramel stream,
Each flavor a whisper, a delightful dream.

I ponder my choices, a cupcake in hand,
Each bite my compass, each crumb is a strand.
The secrets of life baked under soft frost,
With each mouthful savored, my worries feel tossed.

The buttercream wisdom, so smooth and divine,
Suggests that sweet moments are truly the sign.
With laughter and layers, I open my eyes,
To truths hidden deep in the cake's sweet disguise.

So here's to the flavors that dance on my tongue,
With strawberries jiving, and cherries all sprung.
Each dessert a new chapter, each bite a new lore,
As I leap through the frosting, I discover much more!

The Golden Whisk

With a whisk in my hand, I dream of the day,
When batter and wisdom will perfectly play.
I'll mix in some giggles, a pinch of good cheer,
A dash of bright sprinkles, and treasure is near.

Each swirl and each fold brings a tale to the bake,
With secrets emerging in layers I make.
The golden whisk glimmers with truths that I find,
As I whip up my visions, my dreams unconfined.

Flour clouds hug me in a confectionery dance,
While icing on cupcakes provides my romance.
With each twirl around, I feel lighter, it's great,
To learn from my mixing, to savor my fate.

So here's to the moments, with sugar and fun,
With laughter and flavor, my journey's begun.
I'll whisk through my days, leave no batter behind,
For each little treasure's a truth to unwind!

Pastries of Potential

In a world full of pastries, I search for the key,
That unlocks my potential, both frosty and free.
Each croissant a question, each tart a new clue,
With layers of laughter, my confidence grew.

While donuts spin circles, I ponder my fate,
Will I find inspiration while clearing my plate?
With cherry-filled wisdom and éclairs of might,
I nibble on what makes this journey feel right.

The muffins of hope rise up with a grin,
Whisked into dreams of where I will begin.
In every sweet bite, there's a lesson to take,
For it's not just the frosting, but how much I bake.

So here's to the pastries, my gateway to more,
With each tasty venture, I open the door.
In joy and in flavor, I find my own way,
With sprinkles of purpose that brighten each day!

A Sprinkle of Enlightenment

In the kitchen, I ponder, quite deep,
With frosting heights that make me leap.
Oh, to discover what makes me glow,
While raiding the pantry, don't you know?

The chef's hat bobbles, my thoughts collide,
A quest for wisdom mixed with pride.
I spoon up insights, sprinkle them right,
With every bite, comes a new delight.

Baking a pie to map my fate,
As batter flops, I can only wait.
The oven sings a curious tune,
Maybe I should have tried a croon?

Each layer a dream, I stack and serve,
In confection's arms, I find my nerve.
For life's great questions, I take a bite,
With cake and giggles, I feel so light.

Flourishing in Cake

A cupcake with sprinkles, a curious start,
What if dessert is the way to my heart?
As I nibble away, the crumbs fall free,
Perhaps in each bite, I'll find the key.

Frosting whispers secrets, sweet and bold,
In the world of cake, there's treasure untold.
With every mouthful, a laugh breaks through,
Life's a buffet, I'm serving it too.

Muffins rising high, they share my quest,
In their fluffy warmth, I find some rest.
A slice of pie, oh what a ploy,
For finding my bliss, it fills me with joy.

With each new recipe, I dance around,
In flour and sugar, my peace is found.
As I sprinkle life with laughter and cheer,
I mask my searches in icing, my dear.

The Harmony of Sweets

In a bakery's glow, I pause for a chat,
With brownies and tarts, it's where I'm at.
Each slice of cake holds a tale so grand,
Of giggles and sprinkles, all made by hand.

A cookie crumbles with wisdom sublime,
In chocolate chips, I find my rhyme.
Filling doughnuts with laughter's cheer,
Life seems clearer with frosted gear.

Tasting the batter, I'm lost in a dream,
A confectionery swirl, a creamy stream.
While teaspoons of joy rush in like snow,
Each dessert done makes my spirit grow.

With whipped cream mountains and cherry tops,
My journey of fun never quite stops.
In icing and fondant, I find my grace,
Savoring sweetness is my happy place.

The Culinary Compass

A hint of vanilla guides my way,
As I whip up dreams at the close of day.
With spatulas dancing and laughter on cue,
Pastries unravel their wisdom in view.

The oven's warmth holds secrets to share,
In a world of frosting, I take my care.
With pie-crust maps, I search deep in bend,
Each edible treasure becomes my best friend.

Whisking through life with scoops of delight,
Frosted adventures are taking flight.
Cookies are compass points, wide and true,
Leading me onward to ideas anew.

In the flurry of flour, I find my way,
With dessert-filled dreams leading the play.
Each bite a milestone, each layer a song,
In a world of sweetness, I truly belong.

Buttercream Reflections

In frosting dreams, I take a bite,
What am I doing with my life tonight?
Do I seek wisdom or just a snack?
My fork's ambition never looks back.

With every slice, a choice is made,
Is it success or just charade?
Cake crumbs whisper, secrets they keep,
In this sugary quest, I laugh and leap.

Sprinkles of Significance

A sprinkle here, a sprinkle there,
Meaning found in layers of care.
Is this a path or just dessert?
I savor life between each spurt.

Pondering frosting, choices swirl,
Like icing ribbons, life can twirl.
Should I frolic or take a stand?
Oh look! More cake, it's quite unplanned!

The Sweetness of Striving

With each forkful, a quest unfolds,
Purpose baked in chocolate molds.
I rise and fall, like dough in heat,
Does it matter, as long as I eat?

Each bite's a dream, each crumb a chance,
Do I dance with fate, or just eat by chance?
Life's messy like the batter I mix,
But laughter's the frosting, the sweetest fix.

Baked Ambitions

I dream in layers, soft and sweet,
What's next for me? Oh, more to eat!
Goals like cupcakes, frosted right,
But who needs plans when cake's in sight?

With every nibble, doubts dissipate,
Maybe I'll ponder my life on a plate.
But wait, what's that? A slice inviting,
Forget my worries, this cake's exciting!

Patterns in Pastry

In frosting dreams, we carve our fate,
With sprinkles bright, we celebrate.
A buttercream plan, all layered sweet,
With every slice, we try to meet.

We dance with crumbs, a joyous mess,
Each bite we take, more happiness.
The oven beeps, we heat our dreams,
While laughter rises, or so it seems.

Like pie charts round, we slice the air,
In chocolate pools, we dunk our care.
The flaky crust holds secrets tight,
As silly smiles take off in flight.

So grab a fork and dive right in,
In every slice, we find our grin.
With giggles shared and cakes a'plenty,
We whirl in joy, our hearts are merry.

Ganache Goals

With ganache thick, we dream and scheme,
A chocolate river flows like a dream.
We swirl our hopes in rich delight,
With every drop, we lift our flight.

The pastry chef has secret plans,
With butterscotch that twirls like fans.
As candied laughs take center stage,
We're scribbling goals on pastry page.

A slice of pie, a scoop of cream,
We chase our dreams with every theme.
With icing leaping off the edge,
Our confection dreams, we dare to pledge.

In every nibble, wisdom finds,
A cherry on top for thoughtful minds.
Through sugary trials, we rise anew,
Each bite we take, a laugh comes too.

The Layered Expedition

In layers stacked like life's great quests,
We pile on dreams, we take our rests.
With cream and fruit in all their hues,
We ponder life while we peruse.

Each tier a tale, with flavors bold,
In pistachio hopes, we watch unfold.
We scrape the sides, oh what a sight,
While frosting fights our fears by night.

The cake is round, like paths we roam,
With every slice, we're far from home.
A sprinkle here, a laugh exchanged,
Our layered lives are sweetly arranged.

So fork in hand, we share the fun,
In laughter's glow, we've really won.
With every layer, life's twists we take,
We savor moments, bite of cake.

Honeyed Horizons

With honey drips, we toast the day,
Where sunshine meets the sweetest play.
Each golden drop a laugh to share,
As sticky hands brush through the air.

We dip our dreams in pots of gold,
With honeyed wishes, brave and bold.
In every spoonful, stories bloom,
With giggles echoing 'round the room.

The bees buzz softly, whispering cheer,
As we unroll our dreams so dear.
With every taste, our spirits rise,
In sugary trails and honeyed skies.

So let's indulge in moments sweet,
With laughter mixed in every treat.
In sticky fun, we find our way,
With honeyed hearts, we seize the day!

Dusting Off Ambitions

In the kitchen, dreams collide,
With flour clouds and joyful pride.
Mixing hopes in a silver bowl,
Glimpses of a far-off goal.

A single slice, a daring bite,
Sprinkles of laughter, pure delight.
Who needs a map, or even a chart?
Just savor the cake, and play the part.

As I lick the batter from the spoon,
I ponder purpose, night and noon.
With crumbs on my shirt, I rise and grin,
Maybe it's in frosting where I begin.

So here's to the goals that crumble and flake,
Like layers of chocolate in an artful cake.
Three cheers for the fun in this whimsical quest,
Where eating sweet treats feels like the best!

An Invitation to Bake

A party's brewing, come one, come all,
Bring your dreams, let's have a ball!
With eggs and sugar, we'll craft delight,
Baking marvels, a sugary sight.

Forget the stress, leave woes at the door,
Who needs a plan when there's cake to explore?
Whisking laughter, we measure the fun,
Batter and banter, the day's just begun.

In the chaos of sprinkles and pans,
We'll find our calling, amidst frosted bands.
A dash of ambition, a pinch of good cheer,
Together we'll mix, no room for fear.

So grab a spoon, let's embark on this ride,
With laughter and layers, there's nowhere to hide.
Each slice a reminder, as soft as the night,
That finding direction can also feel right!

The Whipped Whispers of Wisdom

Whipped cream clouds in a bowl, so white,
Whispers of dreams take glorious flight.
The voice of the cake calls gentle and sweet,
Inviting us all to take a big seat.

Now mix in some humor, a dash of fun,
Life's puzzles dissolve when ice cream is spun.
With each scoop of joy, a truth comes to light,
Purpose can shimmer like frosting so bright.

As I dig into layers of flavor and flair,
I find all my worries just vanish in air.
For in baking and laughter, one truth comes clear:
The best recipes glow with love and good cheer.

So let's roll the dough and bake up some grace,
With giggles and goodies, we'll find our own space.
Life's sweetest moments come baked and adorned,
In cakes, we discover what we've always yearned!

Pies of Possibility

In my kitchen, dreams take flight,
With flour clouds and sugar bright.
Each slice a hope, a wish in cream,
Baking up my wildest dream.

Sifting through life's endless dough,
Finding flavors in the flow.
Sometimes burnt, but that's okay,
I just add sprinkles, call it a day!

Crusts of courage, fillings bold,
Each pie a story to be told.
With every bite, I seek, I play,
Who knew sweet treats could lead the way?

So let me roll, and let me bake,
Gather joys for goodness' sake.
Life's a feast, a pie parade,
With every fork, new paths are made.

Confectionery Conversations

Over cupcakes and melted frost,
I ponder over dreams now lost.
The frosting swirls, like thoughts that race,
In chocolate, I find my rightful place.

Gumdrops sing, and jellybeans chime,
Whipped cream's sweet, and so is time.
With every nibble, I take a stand,
To live each moment, cake in hand.

Fondant smiles, they whisper low,
What should I do? Where should I go?
With sprinkles scattered, I laugh aloud,
In every treat, I'm joyfully proud.

So let's savor these sugary talks,
As we wander down life's sweet sidewalks.
With laughter and frosting, I sing away,
Life's a candy, every single day.

The Taste of Tomorrow

The clock ticks on, it's time to bake,
I'll whip up dreams like a fluffy cake.
With every layer, I build my fate,
Tomorrow's flavor tastes just great!

Sprinkles of hope on icing so bright,
Velvet dreams, an appetizing sight.
A pinch of courage, a dash of fun,
Baking my path until it's done.

Now that's a filling with zest to share,
Each bite of laughter fills the air.
Looking for meaning in crumbs of cream,
Who knew that truth could taste like a dream?

So let's whisk away what holds us back,
And blend our joys into a happy snack.
Tomorrow's flavors, let them unfurl,
In this cake world, I twirl and swirl!

Flavors of Fulfillment

Life's a buffet of sweet delight,
Like tasting rainbows, oh, what a sight!
With tarts and pies, my heart will soar,
Each little morsel, I can't ignore.

From lemon zest to cherry bright,
With every flavor, I take flight.
I sprinkle dreams in every bite,
Finding joy in every delight.

Let's sprinkle laughter on whipped cream hills,
With cupcakes and giggles, we chase our thrills.
Frosting-fueled, we stumble and glide,
In this cake quest, we take it in stride.

So grab a fork, let's dig right in,
With every dessert, we snicker and grin.
In the flavors of life, we find our thrill,
With sugary smiles, we savor the still!

www.ingramcontent.com/pod-product-compliance
Lightning Source LLC
Chambersburg PA
CBHW051654160426
43209CB00004B/896